rage prayers

rage
prayers

Elizabeth Ashman Riley

morehouse PUBLISHING

Morehouse Publishing, 19 East 34th Street, New York, NY 10016

Morehouse Publishing is an imprint of Church Publishing Incorporated.

Cover design by Paul Soupiset
Flame Image Credit: Gwens Graphic Studio
Typeset by Nord Compo

Library of Congress Cataloging-in-Publication Data

Names: Riley, Elizabeth Ashman, author.
Title: Rage prayers / Elizabeth Ashman Riley.
Description: New York, NY : Morehouse Publishing, [2024]
Identifiers: LCCN 2024013062 | ISBN 9781640657489 (paperback) | ISBN
    9781640657496 (epub)
Subjects: LCSH: Prayer—Christianity. | Anger—Prayers and devotions. |
    Anger—Religious aspects—Christianity.
Classification: LCC BV210.3 .A74 2024 | DDC 242/.8—dc23/eng/20240402
    LC record available at https://lccn.loc.gov/2024013062

For my mom, Kay Josephine Rawlings,

for teaching me how to pray

Contents

Introduction

Welcome to *Rage Prayers*

In many ways my faith journey has defied the odds. Formed in an interfaith family, I found a relationship with the Divine at a young age, pursing the priesthood since I was fifteen years old. While the dominant voice of Christianity in the media continues to be one of exclusiveness, hypocrisy, and judgment, I found my home in the beautiful pocket of a progressive church: not without its own problems, but with a foundation of love and justice that has kept me in relationship with the institution of the church. At the time of this writing, I've spent over decade in ordained ministry, though I do not want to limit this to a Christian conversation, quite the opposite. My deep hope is that everyone can access spiritual practices and a connection with the Holy through the multitude and diversity of faiths that encompass our world.

My experience is unconventional, as many have become disillusioned by religion—particularly Christianity. At the end of the 2010s, there was a 12 percent drop in those who affiliate themselves with Christianity in the United States. At the same time, a growing percentage identify as atheist or a religious "none," compared to the previous decade.* Churches are seeing the real-time impact in shrinking congregations and less cultural relevance. Society yields less and less to the dominance of church schedules on Sunday mornings with extracurriculars and social engagements being scheduled more frequently during what was once traditional church time.

---

* "In U.S., Decline of Christianity Continues at Rapid Pace," Pew Research Center, October 17, 2019, https://www.pewresearch.org/religion/2019/10/17/in-u-s-decline-of-christianity-continues-at-rapid-pace/.

It is not difficult to see how we've gotten here. The invitation into faith is too often accompanied by a denial and repression of the real experiences we face. Positivity has become a toxic tool of manipulation, especially by mainstream and evangelical Christian movements. True experiences are repressed in favor of rose-tinted relationships with the Divine that are rarely more than skin deep. The cognitive dissonance of one's lived experience, both the triumphs and the sorrows, are in dissonance with messages from religion, leaving people spiritually empty.

Even though I am within a branch of Christianity that offers a more nuanced spiritual life, I still grew up internalizing deeply unexamined ideas of right and wrong, good and bad. The black-and-white thinking I inherited, along with the socialization of how I needed to show up as a women, affected my faith. I had a narrow view of emotional and spiritual expression from the church and from the wider society in which I was raised.

During my graduate studies at seminary, I was under observation and evaluation not only for my academic studies but also for my ordination. We were deeply immersed in learning history, ethics, biblical languages, theology, alongside liturgy, pastoral care, and Christian education. On top of all that, we were tending to our spiritual needs, discernment, and paths to the priesthood. I found myself struggling to sink into a rhythm and routine of prayer and practice that was honest rather than performative. Mandatory chapel attendance, prescriptive prayer formulas, and scrutiny of our personal devotions were part of determining our calling and future. Over and over again I failed to stick with a spiritual director, because none of them really connected with how I prayed. I tried out routines and rituals that never seemed to last.

For years I clung so tightly to an image of being right and good that I was suffocating without noticing how thin the air had gotten. My anxiety twisted me into knots that left indelible marks on me, and I was terrified of feeling anything else. It seeped into my spirituality and my prayer life. I struggled to form and maintain a personal practice of prayer that felt authentic to me and "correct" in the eyes of Christians. I found myself constantly wrestling with deeply internalized beliefs around what it was to be "good." This became even more complicated taking on the vows of ordination and serving as a priest in the Episcopal Church.

These unsustainable practices were deeply challenged as the challenges of life piled on. I was inundated with reasons to be angry at God— to express the unfairness and challenges of life. From my dad's cancer and death, my complicated marriage, difficult divorce, traumatic births, casual and aggressive sexism, there has been no shortage of reasons for me to cry and scream at God. Everything doesn't happen for a reason, and this was all a lot.

While my life teetered on the edge of complete unsustainability, our world changed on a global level. The start of our communal awakening, or perhaps dismantling during the pandemic, broke something in me. An unimaginable disease was sweeping the world, pausing our lives and jolting me to my core. Already four months pregnant with my third child and the world shut down. My job both ground to a halt and ramped up, forcing us to master a digital ministry and existence that was draining to say the least. Trapped at home with two small children, a marriage being held together with duct tape, and the absolute exhaustion of my third pregnancy, I had no fucks left. None of this was the plan. I had a plan before all of *this*. This wasn't it.

What the fuck, God?

My body and soul ached. The heart of the world ached. I could no longer catch all the pieces, put on the airs, or keep any sort of facade going. Pieces had to be sacrificed, and I had to let go whether I wanted to or not. I no longer looked like I had it all together. I had to stop caring about what people thought and let the imperfections and the difficulties show. The mask had to drop because there was simply not enough of me to make it all happen. And it was glaringly obvious just how much was supposed to be taken care of by me—for others.

In an offhand moment of vulnerability, I posted a video online to a trending song and invited people to reject the toxic positivity of spirituality so often found in Christianity, and to offer something honest instead. Rage prayers were born. Not just for Christians, but for atheists and seekers, questioners, and other faiths. If we are going to be spiritual, let's at least be honest.

Anger, frustration, rage, and disappointment are not barriers, but connections to God. Our spiritual journeys do not require, and in fact are hindered, by the toxic positivity that is pervasive in religious practices and the modern spiritual movement. God is not a judgmental parent chastising us for being ungrateful or less than perfect. God is not so weak that They need us to constantly fawn over Them to win approval or favor.

What if we fanned the flame of our rage, our anger, not only at the world, but at God? Rage prayers trace the spiritual practice of anger, sanctifying our true experiences and emotions, without caveat. In the process, our connection with God, the Divine, or our spiritual practices are not hindered but deepened. This is not so that we may make a permanent home in our anger, but express it, so we may move through it.

Every generation experiences the evergreen tensions of racial relations, capitalism and economic disparity, violence, and so on. Amid those societal points of friction, our collective, overwhelming anger and sadness begins to combust. Highlighting the failure of existing faith structures and practices, the ongoing nature of our communal and individual struggles demonstrates where we lack the resources to angrily grieve.

This has given way not only to frustration at the failures of our spirituality, but a yearning for something more. People are not walking away from a sense of the Divine, but instead from the structures that have been traditionally in place. Organized religion, as it continues to hold tightly to outdated models, fails to provide a need that is resonating through society. There is a sense of something bigger than us in this life. We seek an expression of the nuance, the bittersweet, the joyful, and the heartbreaking, but are unable to manifest these core tenets of our being while also holding back the truest version of our true selves.

Rage prayers are an invitation to bring the whole self to our spiritual practices. In the messiness of grief, anger, joy, surprise, annoyance, peace, and everything in-between, we simply can't limit what we bring to prayer. Rather than cultivating what feels like the most acceptable version of ourselves in our conversations with God, what if we brought our most authentic selves? Even if that means bringing our doubt, uncertainty, and anger *at* God. What if we brought that to prayer?

This is not a new concept by any means. Lament is woven through Jewish and Christian scripture. The Psalms, Job, even Jesus cries out to God on the cross—"My God, why have you forsaken me?" Our examples of deep emotional expression are as old as any other practice. From art, writing, and music, our feelings have always yearned for a way to be shared, to be known. But through cultural pressure, and institutionalized faith, prayer and rituals have been sanitized, polished, and put forward with their best foot.

Especially in mainstream American Christianity, many prayer practices are presented as blind reverence with shallow praise theology. Perhaps this has been an act of self-preservation. Inviting praise rather than critique, focusing on our own failure and unworthiness without God, and a singular path to salvation by gaining favor with said God is a safe way to keep people invested in the institution. The risk of true feelings—of doubt and anger—could lead to attrition. It could turn people away from God.

There are additional risks of emotional expression that have quieted particular groups of society. Both inside and outside of religion, expectations of how people express emotions has been a means of control and dominance. Women's emotions are policed in a different way than men. The dominant culture will determine what emotional expressions are acceptable and what is dangerous. I recognize that there is privilege in even being able to explore this level of boldness when it comes to emotional expression.

Rage prayers thread an ancient practice into our modern life. It says that whatever or whomever we pray to is big enough to take our full selves, with the anger, doubt, and joy. Incredibly, bringing all of us into our relationship with the Holy might not drive us further away from it, but instead deeper into relationship with the Divine.

This book is an opportunity to pray differently. At the core, it is a rejection of any structures that restrict our experiences of spirituality. It also comes from a particular context and culture. My experience as a white woman certainly shapes how I frame this invitation. There is a privilege I experience in even being able to express anger at God or the injustices I experience. My prayers and my work are informed by my American culture and speak to dominant expressions of religion and society where I am. How this shows up will vary greatly, and expressions of rage, anger, and prayer are contextual to the place where people find themselves. May it help us, in whatever culture we are in, ask questions about our assumptions around prayer, and explore our preconceived notions about connecting with God.

There is no "right" way to read this book, just as there is no "right" way to rage pray. While these prayers are grouped together into sections and themes, it is not a text intended to be read in a linear fashion. Instead, it is a place to turn when a particular topic or theme calls to you. It is a resource and hopefully an inspiration to the prayers you may be holding and need to share with God.

My hope is that these prayers are a springboard for you in your own practice. We all have our own rage prayer inside of us—an authentic conversation with the Divine (or by whatever name you call Them) that we are yearning to have. The only guide is radical honesty. Pray something true. God can handle it.

Raging
through
the
Human
Condition

Faith traditions weave the human condition through the divine experience in intriguing and creative ways. Judaism, Christianity, and Islam all explore this—God coming to understand creation more deeply, and humanity seeking to understand the Divine. In my own tradition of Christianity, God literally takes on this experience that we so often lament. While we fight against our mortality, God joined us in it. It has always been Jesus's humanity—not his divinity—that has captivated me. What does it mean for God to have experienced hunger? Frustration? Exhaustion? In the person of Jesus, God chose the whole of the human condition, joining alongside us in these strange and difficult paths we walk.

As a child I found great comfort in the belief that Jesus was fully human. The idea that he went through everything we did made me feel closer to him. I also took that to mean that Jesus made mistakes and also sinned, just like us. It was comforting to think that I could be imperfect, and that God would understand because of the experience of Christ. In my seven-year-old mind I made sense of salvation by thinking that because God forgave Jesus for his mistakes we were forgiven too. Finding out I was wrong was devastating. Christ's perfection amplified my own shame and imperfection. Not only was Jesus not like me, he was so perfect that even while being fully human he did not stumble. What hope could I possibly have?

To be human is to face the inevitable ups and downs of life. To be human is to mess up. To be human is to fail, and to still be worthy, loved, and cherished. But it comes with the inevitable slog of the experience of life—the triumphs and the failures. There are the familiar experiences that bind us. These same experiences, when addressed in our spiritual lives, are too often swept away with platitudes, blind praise, and distance from raw and tough emotions. Instead, we are taught to focus on the goodness and perfection of Jesus, and to try to be like him; not a small or easy task.

In no small part, this is tied to harmful theological frameworks that connects our success and failures to our favor with God. How many preachers have correlated relationship struggles, addiction, or job loss to an internal failure of spirit? How many people have been shamed and judged into hiding their true experience in the name of making sure God will still love them? How many have experienced rejection because their hardships don't fit with the work of a particular homogenous community? Even when we consciously deconstruct from these beliefs, they are deeply embedded into our culture.

I wrestled with my own internalized beliefs around my value when my marriage fell apart. Especially as I tried to balance my role as a spiritual leader, I questioned whether people would want me in that role given my own failure. I did not know if couples would want me to officiate their weddings, or take counsel from me in their own relationships.

I was confronted with the startling and heartbreaking realization that the mess of my own life was about to spill over into my work. There was no compartmentalizing it, or hiding the shame of it. My humanness would be on display as soon as everyone knew. Would I be blamed for it? Would I be rejected as a spiritual leader because of it? Jesus was perfect (*apparently*) and he was still killed. This does not bode well for fallible human faith leaders.

In the beautiful mess of our lives falling apart, perhaps we can let our theology fall apart as well. It shows the cracks in the structure, and what we have to let go, *because it no longer serves us.* We are not being called to some impossible perfect standard. We are being met where we are by a compassionate God.

Rather than run from struggles and failures, we move through them—lamenting along the way the burdens we bear, those that are unavoidable, and those of our own making. When our prayers can be vulnerable and honest, especially about the truly hard parts of life, there is an opportunity to receive deep compassion. If our prayers repress what is hard, how can we feel anything but shame? Instead, what if we try something different? What if prayer risked saying what we are actually going through and feeling? In that practice I think we have an opportunity to experience something *different*. There we find a chance to acknowledge our shared struggles in this human life while weaving in deep love and relentless forgiveness.

The very public falling apart of my marriage opened up new conversations; they surprised me and renewed my hope. In sharing my grief, others shared theirs. Together we gave space for our sadness and hardships, disappointments and heartbreaks. God's presence was ultimately not in any of the tangible signs of success. It was not made better or stronger when we were more perfect. We did not feel more loved when we fell in line with some artificial good. God's presence and love was made real in the act of vulnerability with one another. It is in these moments of connection, in being in the hard parts *together*, that we find the Divine. That is where we are healed and made new.

Fresh on the heels of my divorce announcement, I joyfully officiated the wedding of a newer couple in my church. For all I feared that I might be an unwelcome guest in joyful celebrations of love, I found quite the opposite. My humanness has not weakened but strengthened the depth of my connections and ministry, and more importantly my connections with the Holy.

There is no shortage of people yearning to be loved, accepted, and supported. There is no shortage of people walking through similar hardships, needing to know that they are not alone in this experience of being human.

We cannot pray away what plagues us, but we can pray into ourselves love, compassion, and strength. We can pray for healing without expecting curing. We can pray for companionship in the muck of life, even if that won't mean escaping it. We can feel seen and heard, even if our prayers are not a magic fix. In that, we might find that deeper connection with the Divine, that truly sustains us through the human condition.

Loneliness

Holy One—

I find myself in vastness.

Be here. I do not want to be alone.

I crave companionship, relationship.

I ache with longing for connection.

The solitude of my experience feels
    insurmountable

And I fear I am the only one who knows this
    disconnect.

Desperately I yearn to break out of this isolation

But it feels impossible and heavy.

I fear the possibility of failing to connect

Of being rejected, of being unworthy

May you be there, with me, in this
    uncomfortable place.

Fill me with knowledge of my wholeness and
    worthiness.
Surround me with Your boundless, unwavering
    grace
That I may know I am your beloved.

Heartbreak

God, this is excruciating,

Why does this reverberate through me?

I do not want to want so hard and so deeply

If I could not care I would,

but I do care and hurt

Which even naming can bring shame

Because I know there are losses that are worse
    than this.

But this loss feels so profound and altering

I do not see the other side of it yet

Be here, in it, with me

Honoring pain, and holding hope

To know that I will survive

Help guide to some other side of this heartbreak.

Parenting Children

Creator and parent of all things,

We cry to you, in the midst

Of fetching snacks, and playing games,

Counseling feelings, and teaching skills,

To hear and see us in the whirlwind of this time.

These tiny humans consume so much of our
    being

The embodiment of our hearts, that we love
    more than words

And to parent them is to know frustration,
    anger, exhaustion, and boredom,

Like nothing else.

Help us to remember and hold fast to our own
selves
As our hearts shatter open to encompass our
love, our anxiety, our hope,
For these tiny precious lives, that we shepherd
them, and not lose ourselves.

Hear our prayer, help us hold onto our sanity,
Keep us afloat, and give us respite to endure,
See and know our thankless sacrifice,
That we may too one day know thanks and
praise for all we have given.

Parenting Teens

Holy One of mystery,
It is an absolute wonder
That humanity has survived
Through the impulsivity of teenagers
Who seem to survive each day by what can
Only be described as divine intervention—

In this time of trial, you test our patience, our
    strength, our resolve,
And we join with you in the practice beyond reason,
Of raising up those who wield great power and
    excitement
While being desperately unaware of their own
    limitations
And sometimes even their own strengths.

Strengthen us, where we stand
That we might not faint at the impossible
And improbable task of ushering
Young people into adulthood.

Give them courage, resilience, compassion, and
    wisdom,
Perhaps give us the same—
That we both may come out of the other side of
    these years intact.

Marriage

Hear our prayer, Spirit of God,
For when we love each other
But don't like each other
For when the little things are really annoying
For when the big things are really hard
And for when we feel stuck in this
And for when we can't breathe
And for when it feels like too much
And for when we are stretched too thin
That we may love each other
Even when we don't like each other

Unfaithfulness

Holiness, I do not feel charitable or forgiving

I do not want to turn the other cheek,

I do not want to rise above.

I want them to hurt, like I hurt.

I want them to feel shame, like I feel shame.

I want them to break, like they broke me.

Is this pain reconcilable? How is this possibly

    healed?

Holiness, hear my prayer, my cry, my pain.

Walk me down the path where I may quench my

    hurt,

And find my way forward.

Divorce

God of Compassion,

I did not pray for this
—until I did.

I prayed every other prayer
—until I prayed this one.

For everything I wanted,
And everything I have,
The time I cannot reclaim,
The sunk cost of all I gave,
The vulnerability I cannot undo,
The other paths I can never explore,
Everything that cannot be brought back,

I grieve as it lays before me,
A mockery and an answer to my prayers.

The weight of loss breaks apart who I was,
My survival coming with irrevocable change
Of both spirit and self.

I am faced with the grief of vows undone.
It would be easier to not believe in vows at all
Than to know they can be broken.

For the easy joy taken, I grieve,
Lamenting the new, unchosen life
That does not yet feel like home.

Job Loss

Almighty—

I need space to just grieve.
How hard, how difficult
How unfair this feels
Before I have to panic
About what comes next.
I am unanchored and angry.
I am tired and weary of this grind.

Quell the wave of shame.

Fill my lungs with air.

Catch me in this free fall.

Soften the edges of indignation

So that I can take the next step forward

And be OK.

Our Bodies

Divine Spirit—
We are formed in human flesh
Embodied in our multifaceted and wondrous
 humanity
But we have failed to love our holy, God-made
 selves
And have fought and battled against our nature
That equips us to do and be—to live in this world.

Rid us of the corrosive, unholy belief that wedges
 between
Us and our love for our holy, sacred, God-made
 bodies.
Strike down the utterly absurd notion
That our value correlates to our size or shape.

For curves and for cellulite, for muscles and for
    wrinkles,
For the parts that shift and the parts that
    change,
For every body in every shape, we give thanks.
May we build up the world to fit every shape and
    incarnation of being
In honor and thanksgiving of the diversity, a
    reflection of God's holiness in the world.
May we delight in our bodies exactly as they are.

Work

There are days it seems utterly ridiculous
That we all are subject to the tedium of work.
For hours and hours and hours we have all
    committed
To doing these things and spending the majority
    of our time
Doing something we would rather not be doing.
And we participate in the continuous grind
    toward
Just allowing ourselves to exist
To have enough to live and survive, let alone
    thrive.

The yolk of capitalism is fierce and exhausting.

Holy One, there must be a better way than this.

Help us make meaning beyond the grind, that
our lives may

Be so much more than a commodity of
productivity.

Depression

Comforter of Your People—
We find ourselves in a place of density and
thickness
Struggling to move through—to want to move
through
The fog of this place, to want to seek you.
It all feels so desperately hard, and we are tired.
We wander, and try to see a way out,
But we are separate from the sparks of happiness
So seemingly effortless for others.
We are exhausted, and the path through is
unclear.

The work forward will be hard,

It would be so easy to sit, and stay awhile, here.

Couldn't you make this all a bit easier?

Lessen the struggle?

Make it lighter?

Holy One—where are you?

Anxiety

Holiness of the multitudes,
Holder of all things,
The unknown swirls within me,
Unsettling my spirit and my soul.
My mind chases itself, seeking a foothold,
Yearning for safety.
The unrest of the unknown and the
    uncontrollable
Nips at my heels and draws my whole focus,
Warping my view, clouding my perspective,
Flooding my being, stealing my joy.

In the grasping for a spot of security,
May you illumine some place where I may pause
Even for a moment—on surefooted ground.
Give me steadiness, soothe my spirit,
And help me find peace.

Soft Landings

God Almighty—
Could you make it a little easier?
I have struggled, and I have fought.
I have faced challenges, I have succeeded, and I
   have failed.
I have celebrated, and I have wept.
Now I need, more than anything, the comfort
   of rest,
A soft landing from where I am, to where I will
   go next,
Some lightening of this arduous journey.
Holy One, hear my prayer,
Give me rest, give me pause.

Addiction

For the Addict

Spirit of Life
This life is hard and I hurt
And I do not want to,
I do not want to be in this.
There is just so much to numb from.
There is so much hurt and pain,
Hardships, and struggles that exhaust us.

Here we find ourselves intertwined,
Both escaping and creating the life
We desperately want to leave
And cannot imagine being away from.

May the warmth of Your love not evade us,
May it seep into our beings,
Take root in our souls and call
Us into lives we yearn to be in.

For the Loved Ones

I am exhausted and angry,
For there seems to be no effort great enough
That any difference is made.
And I am scared.
And I am done, but I am not done
Because how can I be done loving them?
And I cannot know or decide
How to love them and myself
And I hate this thing
And I wish they were stronger

And I wish it were easier

And I pray for them even when

I know they do not pray for me

And I weep with the grief and anger

For this burden and poison entangled with us.

Rock Bottom

The ground is hard and I do not
Absolutely do not
Want to be here.
Finding myself in this place
Consumes me with shame
And I desperately want to turn away
From what lies at the bottom of my self.
My only gratitude is that maybe this
Is the end of my falling
And it cannot get worse—
This is it.

Holy One—you see all of me
Every fault, every misstep
You love me in every form
Love me here—
In this hard place.
Love me here while I cannot love myself
So that I might learn how.
Teach me to stand again.
Show me beyond this moment
My worth and wholeness.

The Grind

Almighty—our lives are not montages.
The details are not swept up into nothingness
But found in the day in and day out
Of grinding effort,
Sometimes overwhelmingly inescapable.

The incredibly boring minutia of every day,
The hard, slow work of each step of effort
To exist in our imperfect world
Is enough to suck out any care we could give
Toward a bigger care in the universe.

May the grind not wear too deep.
Leave our souls intact so that
We might give a damn.

What's Next

There is a question so often asked of us
When we are in the liminal of in-between
Of which direction our paths are headed.

For the times when we know beyond a doubt
Stand with our certainty.

When we waiver,
    bend with us.

When we freeze,
    hold tight.

When we turn,
    stay close.

When we roll our eyes at those
More interested in being spectators of our
 journeys
Rather than companions on the road
Smirk with us.

In the knowing and unknowing what's next
Let us find ourselves in the being rather than the
 defining.

Underarppreciated

Holy One—
For those whose toils are never noticed,
Whose contributions are unseen,
Who do not hear enough thanks,
We pray.

For praises unsung,
For talent undervalued,
We pray.

For repentance of a society
That demeans the wisdom and strength
Of the overqualified
In favor of familiar mediocrity
We pray.

For the nameless who have contributed
And given to what and who we are
But we will never know,
We give thanks.

For those who willingly worked before us
Who fight for the unseen and unknown,
And give voice to the voiceless,
We give thanks.

Raging
at
Mortality

While my dad lay in the hospice bed that was set up in our shared apartment, oxygen running, medication dulling the pain and his mind, I snapped at my grandmother. She has ventured into his room, after I told her not to, waking him up. At twenty-six, I was the full-time primary caregiver for my dying father. I mentally calculated what was needed to help him settle enough to go back to sleep (medication, water, and comfort care). I admonished her for her carelessness at disturbing him. She stomped her cane on the ground between us, looking me in the eye: "I was there when he opened his eyes for the first time: I can go in his room. I am his mother." Her sweet southern drawl cut with finality.

She would go on to pray, as she had since his diagnosis, sitting vigil by his bedside. She would often give the nurses suggestions, or ask questions, citing her own background as an Air Force nurse years ago. Sitting and fussing over him, she would pray that God would save him, and she prayed for a miracle. For the fifteen months he battled cancer she told me we just had to have enough faith, and I eventually stopped arguing with her about the nature of prayer. He died a few days later, just twelve days short of my ordination as a priest.

It is part of our human nature to fight against our mortality. The fragility, and singularity of our lives, has driven us forward, advancing medicine, science, propelling our evolution and our drive. But we have not defeated death. We share in the common experience across cultures, religion, and time, of the nature of our one lifetime. We share within it the vulnerabilities of our human, embodied selves, and the exquisite joys that can accompany it.

Frequently, our faith practices are particularly built around longing and desire to make sense of our mortality. Where do we come from? Where do we go when we die? How do we make sense of the unexplainable? There is good and faithful work on these questions in every culture and branch of religion. There is also an incredibly amount of sloppy and shallow theology that does so much more harm than good. Everything doesn't happen for a reason; it's not all a part of God's plan. Aliments are not divine punishments, and God never—NEVER—needs another angel.

I showed little tolerance for platitudes of faith after my dad passed away. People were quick to assume that as a Christian I would want to hear that it was all part of God's plan. Nothing could be further from the truth. This was not the first or last loss in my life, and a belief that any of that is part of some master plan is wildly discomforting.

I never spoke much with my grandmother about her faith after my dad died. I wonder what it left her with—if she just told herself, it was part of God's plan or that God had their reasons. There is no loss like the loss of a child.

The grief she had to step into is excruciating. I do not blame her for whatever she grabbed on to in order to survive. But I wonder where she was left short, where her theology failed to make sense of this cataclysmic loss.

The blatantly abusive way in which salvation has been used to coerce and control people is a deep wound of the past and present. Mortality has been leveraged against people by the very institutions that are supposed to help us understand a holy, loving God. Rather than instilling peace, religion has often left people more fearful or even distant from God. If we can only be close with God when our lives are good, how are we supposed to survive when things are hard?

Our faith might not explain away the bad things. Letting go of those platitudes can mean letting go of comfort and security that protects and sustains us in dark and difficult times. It means stepping onto unfamiliar ground. It might invite us to be angry at God. It might cause us to doubt our faith. It might cause us to do some soul searching. That vulnerability is the key to it making any difference at all. If there is nothing risked, then there is little to be gained.

My father's death was devastating. It irrevocably changed my life. It is not something that I need to make palatable to fit into my spiritual beliefs. I am still surprised as people who try to twist the narrative of his death into a divine plan, especially when it comes from other spiritual leaders. There doesn't need to be a reason or purpose behind it. It is allowed to be awful. Anything less feels disingenuous, both to his life, his loss, and even to God. I would have little respect or praise for a god that micromanaged health and miracles in such cruel ways. My faith does not explain away his death, or cancer.

God cannot turn back the clock or remove my pain. They are not punishing my dad or me or anyone else by failing to give divine intervention.

What God can be is a companion. A place to help hold the earth-shattering loss and emptiness that accompanied my grief. I do not have to be in my grief alone, and I do not have to deny my loss in order to maintain my faith—the two can coexist.

What faith can offer is a companionship in the dark and difficult times. It can be an outlet for our pain, our frustration, our fear. The ways in which our bodies fail to perform the way we want them to—the challenges they present, those are worthy things to rage about. In the Christian tradition, we believe that God became incarnate in human flesh and experienced the same mortal trials and tribulations that we do. Our incarnate God died at human hands. Perhaps God knows something about raging at mortality.

Illness

Eternalness—you formed us in limited, wondrous,
    holy, imperfect bodies,
Filled with possibilities and limitations,
Fragility and susceptibility sometimes caging,
Limiting our lives.
What sense does it make in the design of your
    world to limit us, afflict us?
How much easier it would be without all of this
To contend with on top of every other struggle
    of the world?
God, hear the prayers,
The rage, the grief.
For the loss of time and energy,
For everything that is that much harder,
And everything that can't be had.

For bodies that struggle, and fight, and are
    exhausted,
For the fear, the cost, and the work,
For lives longed for, and dreams unrealized,
We weep.

Cancer

God,

Fuck cancer.

Infertility

Great Creator,

You birthed creation and us,

Forming us and bidding us to be cocreators

    with you,

Planting within us the wanting and hope of that

    promise.

You greet our longing with emptiness.

The utter unfairness

And ridiculousness of biology

Mocks the calling toward parenthood

For those who deeply want but cannot have.

At odds with ourselves and with you
At odds with all that we hope for, all that we
    dream of
We cry and lament,
We scream and grieve,
For that which feels out of reach
For the suffocating want
For our unfilled lives
We cry to you.

Childbirth

Mother God,
You bore all of creation,
Pouring yourself out into the world.
The pains of childbirth
Ripple through the generations,
Exposing our culture's values and hopes
And too often lack thereof—
For the ones who bring forth new life.
The burden of this work
Rips us apart, offering up ourselves
In agony and in joy with a task
Unequally yoked upon the bodies of some.

May their cries bear witness to what they risk
—the extraordinary, excruciating, and enormous
task
Of birthing life in the world.
Holy One, be with them in their pains and joys,
Companion them alongside the witness and
strength
Of those who have come before, and those who
will come after,
Cocreators with you, of our wondrous humanity.

Miscarriage

The shattering of tender hope
In a loss that can be so shrouded
In stories of miracles of new life,
We cannot find ourselves.
God may we be met in
The liminal space of life,
Seeking out our tangible grief
Of that which was, which could have been
The loss of a reality and of a future
That we may know the fullness of that loss
Because of the fierceness of our love that came
    with it.

Death of a Child

It is not right,
It is unfair and outrageous,

But it is.

And this unthinkable, unimaginable thing,
Is one that we must live through.

And we walk this unfathomable path
That no one should have to face
In desperate loneliness, rage, and anger.
Part of ourselves lost in their absence,
The chasm of loss between where we are and
Everything that we had and had imagined
        would be.

Oceans of grief, of anger, of lost hope, crash
    over us,
A world so fundamentally changed,
A naivety of self never to be found again.

Holiness, Divine One,
Be strong enough, for our anger, our grief,
Our rage, our pain, to know who we are now
Without.

To calibrate to a world forced upon us
That we might choose to be in it
And still know you,
That we might still be and know that they were.

Chronic Illness

O Healer of the Multitudes,

Where are you as I suffer here?

I am deeply aware of the burdens I bear,

Watching others live with ease where I do not.

The constant, endless drum of this that I battle

That I cannot escape but am forced to bear

Chips away at my resolve and my soul.

I seek your relief for a burden I cannot set down
   or share.

For the effort and endurance, for the life I
   suffer for

I beg that you give me just some of the ease

That everyone else takes for granted

While I continue to labor for my existence.

Terminal Illness

It feels so arbitrary that there are illnesses we just
    cannot conquer
—that there is nothing we can do.
That of all the illnesses we can make well, this is
    not one.
Even though we all will eventually die,
This feels *so unfair.*

We weep. We rage. For our helplessness,
For all that will go unfinished, we mourn.
For what is left, time that is laced with
        knowledge and finality.

God, why did you design humanity,
With such ridiculous flaws,
Sentencing us to random and unfair lives?

Why, O God?

The Cost of Care

God of Justice,
power of the marginalized,

We've capitalized compassion,
Contorting our very ability to love one another
And meet our basic human dignity.

For our disgusting human practices
That so clearly show the gap
Between our wealth and our love of one another,
    we repent.

Return us to one another with compassion.

Renew our mutual care and joy at our mutual
flourishing.

Reject our corruption and our greed.

May we remember that one another's precious
existence

Is beyond any monetary price to be gained.

Obligatory Caregiving

Our Great Confessor,
I do not want to care anymore,
To do this work and take on this task,
That I did not want or ask for,
But have nowhere else to put it.
And I grieve and rage and lament,
At all I have to relinquish and pour out,
Of time and resources,
    of everything that goes undone,
And all I do not have, so that I can do this.
And I deeply wish I could walk away
And leave this to someone else.
Know our suffering and our shame,
For this burden we must carry.

Caregiving

Creator, the task of caring, of loving and managing, even when deeply rooted in love— but especially when fulfilled out of necessity and obligation—is a heavy weight. For all that we pour out, so little is poured back into us. As our lives are intrinsically tied together, the task of caring for one another falls in unbalanced ways. For that grief, this task, for seemingly endless roads ahead, and ones that are unflinchingly final and unavoidable, we pray. For our grief at this burden, for the possibilities for ourselves that are lost, we lament. Be with us in the complexity of love and grief, of sacred and burdensome tasks, that we may not feel them alone.

Death

Holy One, the finality of death envelopes us
Even with our faith—our hope—in something
    more.
It knocks the air out of us as life is irrevocably
    changed.

Death is cavernous, reverberating our grief and
    our gratitude.
For the end of suffering, we are asked to sit with
    our desperation,
Our desire to undo the loss, our relief for the end
    of suffering,
Our surprising happiness, and the loneliness
    that surrounds us

In death—our own, our loved ones,
May we find you in the multifaceted nature
Of fear and hope, anger and joy
To companion us and all we feel,
Walking this unknowable path
That we may not be alone.

Grief

Almighty Spirit,
This is a pain I could not have known
Before a loss like this.
And the weight of it
Feels unbearable.
I cannot shed its burden
And sadness suffocates anger.

Give breath to that which cannot be squashed
But only moved through,
Grief undiminishable yet torturously survivable.

And we clamber laboriously forward,
Surrounded by the saints who share the losses of
    love,
Bearing witness to the grief,
Companions in pain
And beacons of futures
Forever changed by loss,
But themselves not entirely dimmed.

Inconvenient Grief

God—could you just—
Not.

It's enough to know the depth of loss

But incredibly annoying that
It shows up whenever it pleases.

If you would not intervene in
Matters of life and death

Perhaps this you could make
Just slightly less obnoxious,
And allow our grief
To be more compartmentalized.

Raging
with
Faith

At its best, faith in something bigger than ourselves instills a sense of purpose, serenity, love, and acceptance. It helps us make sense of the world and our place in it. We are aligned with our values and our purpose when we live into our faith and within the structures that help us support that faith. These same structures can also take that alignment, that love for the Divine, and make obedience and devotion the overarching message.

Love for God comes in many ways. It develops sometimes out of genuine gratitude and devotion that fills us up. It also develops out of fear: fear of punishment, fear of rejection, fear of failing. A love for God can become a blind, unquestioning obedience. Faith can make our lives fuller and brighter; it can also narrow and dim our lives.

My maternal great-grandmother, a devout Catholic, infamously had all her dental work done with no numbing agents or pain medication in order to repent for the sins of her children. An act of love, I suspect, for them, and for God. I heard this story for years before knowing she lost two of her six children. One to meningitis and one to a faulty light in the 1920s when electricity in homes was still new. I wonder how her faith helped hold her together with such grief. I wonder if Mary's grief gave her comfort and strength as a fellow mother.

My own mother went to Catholic school, and the nuns with their habits and veils were so intimidating and scary she ran away during lunchtime on her first day of school. She was the youngest of seven, and Catholicism didn't seem to stick with any of them. Only her eldest sister tried to claim it despite rarely attending Mass. She did, however, insist that she would need last rites from a real Catholic priest, not me.

Institutions of faith have left indelible marks on practices of faith that we are left to make sense of. We have to deconstruct our beliefs, values, and preconceived notions so that we might get to the truth of the matter. We need to scrub clean the system of God as dictator and authoritarian. We need to untangle the very human voice of control that has seeped into our practices and been falsely anointed. Any love that is unable to be challenged—unable to be vulnerable to the whole host of our feelings and being—that is not actual love. God should be able to take some scrutiny. Our faith should be able to take some scrutiny.

During our family's reentry to spirituality, Dad attended the reform synagogue in town, exploring the faith that had been his own father's even though he himself had not been raised Jewish. Mom attended the Catholic Church, returning to what was familiar from her own childhood. My sister and I worshiped with both faith communities. When I was seven, I asked to be baptized while my sister chose our Jewish heritage.

I loved the church, its beauty and comfort. I loved getting donuts at coffee hour and getting dressed up for worship with my mom. I loved our routine each night when I got into the top bunk and my mom would pray with me, teaching me the Lord's Prayer and the Hail Mary. I still went to synagogue with my dad and sister, but church felt like home.

I cannot remember the priest of that church who rarely interacted with the children. Our spiritual leader was Sister Mary Margaret, a woman who radiated God's love, and who I adored. I'll never forget her excitement when she announced to us that girls could serve as altar boys, not even having a word yet for what we could be. I was disappointed, not knowing we had ever been barred from doing it, and confused at why that had been.

After my baptism, I dutifully prepared for first communion, as is the tradition in the Catholic Church. In Sunday school we were learning its significance, its *necessity*, for our salvation. I beamed with pride to partake in the sacrament—until I learned that my mother would no longer be allowed to receive it as well. Through the convoluted rules of divorce and remarriage, her options were limited. To my seven-year-old self the answer was clear—we would go to a different church. If communion was so important, then we couldn't stay here. Despite her offers to stay, I insisted we leave.

I'm not sure my Sunday school teachers could have imagined the way I would internalize their teachings. I accepted Jesus, communion, all that felt true. In fact, I'm surprised that I took the sacrament so seriously. I wanted to be in a relationship with God, and I knew deeply that I was loved. I had faith in what I had been taught, and I wanted to find a church that let us fully experience that.

It would take years of being without a congregation before we stumbled into the Episcopal

Church, trying various other churches until we found the one that was just right. In hindsight I'm startled by the trust and bravery my mom showed in her faith. She modeled something unique, and trusted in God in ways that few people can. She and my dad allowed us to wander and explore. They allowed us to choose different paths for ourselves. My sister's interest in the temple deepened our dad's engagement as well. At the heart of what they did right was allowing us to be our full, authentic, unique selves, and supporting whatever direction that took us.

What is available to us when we live into a faith that allows us to bring our whole selves to the table? What if we say the quiet parts out loud? The things we are never encouraged to talk about. The laments that we are supposed to keep hidden or private? What if our pain and our grief wasn't indecent but holy? What if we could still love God even when we are incredibly mad at God? Perhaps that comes with risk. But there is also something incredible possible when we are open to that risk.

In my life, the holiest relationships are least inhibited. The people who have witnessed me at my best and my worst, and have continued to love me, are the most sacred. These are the relationships that are able to grow and evolve, that transform with challenge, and can stay rooted in the deepest love for one another. These are the relationships that sustain me. That is the relationship I want with the Divine. That is the place where I want to meet God. To know I am loved at my best and at my worst.

Doubt

In the depth of others' certainty,

I find only questions and doubt,

Weaving a circuitous path between

What may—or may not—be the Holiness,

The weight of doubt and unknowing

Cast as a wedge of superiority toward

Those whose faith is unwavering.

I wonder at what that knowing feels like.

I long for such grounded faith,

But my questions are unsatisfied.

I am left restless, unable to settle for

Shallow answers amidst the depth of mystery.

Sanctify my doubt,

That it may not be cast away for inconvenience

But embraced for what it illuminates,

For the sacred path it illuminates.

May the yearning to quench our curiosities

Take us ever closer to the Holy.

Weaponized Faith

For each verse of holy words
That we have sharpened into daggers,
We repent.

For the blood they've drawn,
For the scars they've left,
We repent.

For rituals under the guise of belonging
That we used to exclude,
We repent.

For sacred spaces used
To coerce obedience,
We repent.

For the irrevocable harm
Between people and God at the hands
Of those false prophets who abused
The name of the Divine,
We repent.

Absent God

To the unanswering heavens I shout,
Despite not knowing the voice of comfort
So many others speak of hearing,
Despite my calls to you.

For the Divine to whom I have gone
without introduction,
A closeness I crave but is not realized,
I pray.

I have shouted words into the abyss,
Pleaded into the night,

Praised in the morning,
In my need and in my despair
sought your wisdom at crossroads,
But I do not hear your voice.
I seek, and do not find your steadfast presence.
Holiness—if you are there,
Hear my prayer.

Unanswered Prayers

Holiness,
In faithfulness I have cast my prayers,
Petitions and pleas,
Offering my praise and thanksgiving,
Opening my heart and bearing my prayers
To you.

But for the prayers I have lifted to your name
In hope of something changed go unanswered.

I am left to wonder if my prayers anger you,
Or are unworthy of answering?

And I wonder what is the point of praying
        at all,
If I am shouting into the wind?

Lost Faith

To the God I once prayed to,
And now cannot quite name,
To the Holiness that brought me comfort,
But now I cannot feel,
To the Divinity I was certain in,
And now cannot find,
I lift up this prayer.

I cannot find the steadiness
Of your presence that others proclaim
And that I once knew.

The absence of your being
Reverberates throughout my life,
The promise of You elusive and hollow,
A chasm between the Divine and me.

To the Divine that I'm uncertain is there—
Hear my prayer.

Questioning

Almighty God—
How can others be so certain,
When there are so many questions?
In the midst of your professed Truth
That so many others proclaim,
We find a multitude of questions
Itching at our souls—wondering,
Doubting, seeking, and challenging.
Anoint that which is unknown.

Release us from the duality that gives

Us a singular right

And instead find you in the multiplicity

Of nuance, the unknown, that

You may be found not in the answer but in the
asking.

Toxic Positivity

Our oversimplification

Of the Divine

In the fear of the unknown—

Too often shapes our theology

Around false ideals,

Of almighty holy plans and our own blind hope.

Rather than give weight

To the unknown of it all,

Or our fear, anger, sadness, and so on,

Our theology has been boiled down

To the cookie-cutter shape of shallowly following.

May we smash the confinements of false
    optimism
To relinquish all that we feel—whatever it may
    bring,
Trusting you to hold—all of it.

False Prophets

Draped in promises and hope,
Salvation is touted by many
Using Your name, manipulating Your hope,
Warping Your promise.

My God, why do you allow
So many to hurt and abuse
In your name?

Where is your power to quell the voices
Of those peddling poison
And calling it miraculous?

Lamenting, raging, we cry
Against the wounds born by the innocent
At the hands of false prophets
And the chasm they wedge
Between humanity and the Holy.

Purity Culture

Despite our holy creation
Embodied in flesh,
Our world has raged war
Against our sacred selves,
Controlling, shaming, and demonizing
Our bodies, twisting the words of God,
Dividing us from our very selves,
Seeding within us doubt of our
Beauty and worth.

May we repent of the scars left on our world from
Slut-shaming, purity, and
Corrosive control of our divine bodies.

May we who bear these scars

Shake loose the visible and invisible hold

On our minds and bodies,

And pray we can love our whole selves and
bodies

As God created and intended.

The Harm
of Salvation

In trying to drive people to you with fear
Through hope of eternal life and in fear of
    salvation,
We have broken so much faith and trust.
We have ripped people from God's love
And replaced it with judgment that is soaked
In human construction and yet named as God's
    will.
May our churches repent of the corruption
Twisted out of God's dream of eternal life.

May we shed theology that has abused God's
     people.
May we risk a relationship with God that does not
Force our obedience but invite a way of life
Steeped in grace.

Indoctrination

For us who drank from the cup
Of beliefs without choice or option,
Where questions were silenced
And belief weaponized,

We pray that you might help us
Untangle everything we were indoctrinated to,
From our understanding of ourselves and the
     world,
To shed that which does not serve us,
To have the bravery to ask questions,
And to break from all we've known.

In the midst of exhaustion and grief,
To know you will not abandon us
No matter how far we must wander
To find our own selves and beliefs—
Because it is there you have always known
Us and love us from the beginning
For exactly who we are and not what we profess.

White Jesus

For the mockery of Christ found in the
    whitewashed king,
Who is only a faint reflection of the Jesus of
    Nazareth,
The one who walked the Holy Lands,
We repent.

For the arrogance that bore forth the church
    that has
Separated Christ from humanity by demanding
    his whiteness,
For how it has stripped and sanitized him of not
    only his identity,
But humanity and divinity,
We repent.

For Jesus sits among the marginalized,

Whose skin is anything but pale,

Whose hope is anything but mild,

And whose justice is anything but quiet,

We hope, and we pray.

Silencing Women

Mother God,
For every woman told not to speak,
For her voice that went unheard,
For her words that were not shared,
For her songs unsung,
For her story that was not told,
We pray.

We look back through our stories
To see the women threaded through history
Who were minimized or forgotten,
Silence and downtrodden,
For our foremothers,
We weep.

For the fear and oppression,
For the power and the dominance
That have tried to keep us small and quiet,
We rage.

And we hope
For every voice that has defied
And fought and shouted and whispered
And fuel and unquenchable truth.

Harming the Marginalized

Almighty God,

You have always seen those who society casts out
and puts at the margins.

You have taught us to love them and care for
them.

And despite your message

Our institutes of faith continue to harm those
you love

In what is done and left undone.

We have lost touch of our common humanity
with one another

And left the marginalized to bear the weight of
that harm.

For those who have been left and forgotten, we
    pray,
That they may know your hope despite the
    failures
Of those who act in Your name.
Illumine the hypocrisy of faith, that our
    institutions
Might reconcile message and action
To align with your love
And care for those on the edges of our
    communities to draw
Them in, disrupt the borders of our communities
And embody the kingdom that we hope for.

Raging
for
Justice

The summer before I started high school, there was a highly publicized hate crime involving teenagers shooting paintballs at indigenous unhoused people. The case sparked national attention, and fueled conversations and legislation around hate crimes in Alaska. My dad was the presiding judge on the case, receiving his own criticism and public attention. His labeling of the case as a hate crime, and his invitation of the indigenous community to speak to its impact on them, caused significant reactions. He publicly critiqued the judicial system and its failure, saying of himself and the prosecution and defense attorneys that "three middle-aged white guys" should not be the primary voices in this trial. Maybe it was because I was old enough to notice, but this case came home with him more than any other.

The morning of the sentencing I made him breakfast. I was grateful that this whole ordeal would be over soon, and I wanted to be a source of comfort for him, even though I couldn't fully grasp what he was going through, or why it was so significant. Later that day, I watched clips of it on the news. The piercing look and measured voice he used to explain to the defendant the consequences of his actions were familiar. The gravity of his quiet speech was more difficult to listen to than shouting. I knew the deep respect I held for his opinion, and for what he modeled. He had the privilege of one who could choose not to engage or speak out. He had the privilege of being male and white. He chose not to look away. He chose to critique the system that supported his authority. I learned not to look away, though I have not always lived up to that teaching or his example.

If you're paying attention, your heart is probably breaking. There is no shortage of suffering and injustice in the world. In fact, to really try and take it all in can be incredibly overwhelming. How can we possibly make any difference in all of these things? How can our world be so broken? How can there be so much suffering?

The magnitude of need is paralyzing. No wonder we turn to something bigger than ourselves to make sense of it all. Time and again religion has failed to truly show up in the face of crisis. More often than not, religious institutions continue to prop up suffering and oppression while preaching the love of God. The hypocrisy has driven plenty of people away, not only from organized religion but spirituality altogether.

When our institutions of faith cannot give us anything tangible in the face of the world crying out for justice, we can see the flaws in our systems of belief. We send our "thoughts and prayers" and leave the world in more pain, with nothing changed. It turns our "thoughts and prayers" into a hollow joke—a Band-Aid to slap over the world's pain.

Once we let go of any idea that events are preordained, or that it's all part of God's plan, the ground doesn't feel very sturdy. It is unfamiliar territory to step into a faith structure where we try to stop seeing God as the puppet master, intervener, or wish granter. It is uncomfortable to fully see the world's suffering and to take in how unfair it all really is. Only then we might be shaken enough to go beyond leaving it all in God's hand. It is not a magical solution from outside of us that we need. We are the solution. We are the change makers.

Justice can never stop at "thoughts and prayers." It demands our action, for us to show up in the world, and shape it to give dignity to all of creation. "Thoughts and prayers" are not the ending, but the beginning. They are the fuel that pushes us to see, to not turn away from the brokenness around us.

We rage *for* justice. We feel the hurt of the world, we name it, and we step forward to change it.

The Episcopal church that I first found was a truly special place: progressive, loving, and quirky. They practiced what they preached, and demonstrated how faith could support our need for justice and healing in the world. My passion and audacity led me to church leadership despite my young age. The church wove my care for the dignity of all people with a welcoming, loving community.

At the time, on a national scale, the Episcopal Church was debating gay rights, particularly the inclusion of queer clergy as ordained leaders. The idea that someone's God-given identity could make them somehow less worthy was completely contrary to the gospel—which seemed clear to me. We should not debate the dignity and worth of another human being. The message of Christ was obvious: love everyone. Care for the suffering. Don't be a jerk. We entered this conversation only a few years after the highly publicized hate crime against Matthew Shepard, a young man who was brutally murdered for being gay. He had been Episcopalian and an acolyte in his church.

At fifteen, I served as an elected, voting representative at our regional gatherings that governed the Episcopal Church in the state of Alaska. I sat with other gathered leaders to vote on the budget, participate in Bible study, and do the business of the church. It felt like a beautiful blend of impactful business and faithful devotion.

A priest there, who I do not remember much about except that he was white and male, vehemently opposed the inclusion of queer clergy. His reasoning included that it would lead to polygamy and polyamorous relationships. I was enraged. His lack of Christianity and compassion was antithetical to the gospel. His argument used weak and faulty logic that the debate student in me could not ignore. I did not hesitate in explaining to him how bad his argument was on both a spiritual and logical level.

At the end of the day, we came together for an evening service (called Compline in our tradition). We clustered into pews and gathered for prayers—the priest I argued with, alongside everyone else. We all had spent the day voicing dissenting positions from one other. We argued over money, and scripture, and ethics, and procedure. And we all still came here and held hands and prayed—siblings in Christ. We did not need to agree. Our differences were not nullified or hidden. Our connection and our relationship, knit together in our prayer and faith, was big enough for our differences and our commonalities.

I knew in that moment that what I was experiencing, this place of prayer even in conflict, this thing that was big enough to hold us together in difference, that was something I wanted more of. This was something I wanted for the rest of my life. The next morning I found my own priest in the crowd of gathered leaders and I told him I wanted to go into ministry. I never knew anything but heartfelt support from my leadership as I was raised up for ordination.

The debate over queer inclusion in the church has not been easy, and the battle for justice isn't over inside or outside of the church. But there are pockets of hope. When hate crime legislation was passed in 2009, it was named after two people, including Matthew Shepard. Twenty years after his death, once his family felt that his safety could be ensured, his final resting home was made at the National Cathedral. The service for his interment was presided over by Bishop Gene Robinson, the first openly gay bishop ordained in the Episcopal Church.

The hope that things can be better, *should* be better, is a subversive hope. It defies the odds to believe that a system too heavily favoring those already in power might ever change to truly support and care for the marginalized. This is the work of faith. It forces us to remain unsettled when the praying is done. It makes us face the suffering we might want to turn away from. It drives us to keep trying to make things different. Perhaps we cannot fix everything. But we can change some things— and that is worth doing.

White Nationalism

We name the evil of white nationalism,

Its presence in our communities,

In our society, and in our houses of faith.

Let us not turn away from truth or let shame

stop us in right action

To call out the arrogance manifest as violence,

unholy, and unjust.

We repent of the destruction and discrimination

The dehumanization and violence justified for its

means.

We name its pervasiveness in our world.

May we not be silent in the presence of

dehumanization.

Hold us accountable to our action and our

inaction.

Elections / Politics

Holy One, everything around is turned upside down in the name of elections. Our politics and our processes are so far from what hurting people in the world need. The cost of time, the cost of energy, the cost of money, is an appalling reflection of the values of our country. The system is broken, and somehow we are supposed to make the best of it. God, we long for something different, where justice may roll forth, where we can break free of the hold of what no longer serves us.

Holy One, show up in the midst of our fights for justice, strengthening those who continue to stand against impossible odds, in the hopes that we might do something different, and create a world that cares and supports all people. Holy One, may we not lose hope.

Gun Violence

God of peace, once again, we find ourselves
in the shadow of gun violence, praying to you.

Our bodies, minds, and spirits
are filled with rage and anguish.

Your beloved children, our beloved children,
have been victims of violence that cannot be
    undone
—and we pray for their comfort and rest in your
    endless love.

Be with those who weep most deeply,
may their grief be met with your tenderness and
    your presence.
May none grieve alone.

As you witnessed the death of your son,
so too do we witness these deaths,
and we despair at the unceasing violence and hate
that courses through the world.

May our lament, and anguish, that feels
        uncontainable,
burn into something new: a spirit of justice and
        peace,
that does not settle for the world as it is,
but envisions the kingdom of God as you have
        promised,
and as you've equipped us here and now to make
        real.

Let our tears plant deep the seeds of this kingdom,
of peace and justice, where we create for us and
        all your children,
the world of peace as you have promised,
and as we are called to build.

May we remember that one who was and is and
    is to come,
and know the hope of that coming, even in the
    despair of this moment.

In your loving name, Mother, Son, and Holy
    Spirit, we pray: Amen.

Racism

We are compelled, O Holy One, in confession
    and repentance,
To confront the human sin of racism, often
    shrouded and protected,
Through the people and institutions wielding the
    holy name of God.
The history and wounds so deep and broad, the
    work ahead severe.

For all that has been broken, stolen, and
    destroyed from this sin, we lament.
For the divisions and walls that have been built
    between the children of God, we pray.

For our own inherent othering, our prejudice,
   our judgment, we repent.
For a path forward, of reparations of
   reconciliation to you, God, we hope.

Climate Change

Creator of all things—
Our greed, our consumption, and our
    self-absorption,
Has wounded this holy planet.
We have avoided and denied accountability,
Carrying more about our own self-interests
Than that of all of humanity and creation.

We weep for the Earth and the damage we have
    caused,
For the extraordinary life you have infused into
    the world
In plants and creatures, all forms of life and
    creation
That we have treated so carelessly.

We fear for the future, for ourselves,

For the generations to come, and the mess they
inherit.

We repent for our failure, for our consumption,
for our arrogance.

We pray for the healing of the world around us

For the healing of ourselves, that we might turn
our hearts

Toward care and stewardship of the whole Earth.

War

Holy Spirit—we are embroiled in terror and
   violence.
The world is enraged, the world is on fire,
And the lives of innocents lost and destroyed
While powerful people argue, and others suffer
—we bear witness, we mourn.

For our love of power over our love of people,
We repent.

For our failures, the dehumanization, and
   selfishness,
We repent.

For the innocent and the complicit who suffer,
Who lose their lives,
We pray.

We pray for enemies, and we pray for friends,
For our shared humanity
Must be greater than any conflict of control.

We pray that the dignity of all people be never
    compromised,
Or forgotten.

Genocide

Source of Goodness and Life,

We do not look away from the darkness of
humanity.

We see our faces reflected in the humanity of
those who suffer.

We see our faces reflected in the humanity of
those who oppress.

We do not forget the actions and the evil
perpetrated.

We do not justify the dehumanizing and othering.

We will remember lives lost,

The peoples and nations decimated.

To the cultures erased and the heritage lost,

We recognize our global complicity and our
failures to act.

We wrestle with the darkness of humanity, the
darkness within ourselves.

We will not minimize the destructive power of
hatred.

We will not fail to stand and name this evil when
it's present.

We will not fail to stay with those who cannot
flee its crushing presence.

Islamophobia

For the children of Allah,
For their bright faith,
For their beautiful witness,
We pray.

For the othering of God's children,
We repent.

For their sacred lives lost,
We lament.

For the living faith of Islam,
We give thanks.

That our ignorance might be lessened,

That our minds might be opened,

That we may reverently protect and honor

The faith and dignity of those we

May not know or may not understand.

That we may learn from them something of

     God's love,

We pray.

Antisemitism

God of our Ancestors, Holy One, in our desire to praise your name, we have trampled our siblings, we have used them, and turned against them, for our own gain. Our words, our attitudes, our teachings have profoundly harmed the Jewish people, and we have failed to honor your covenant with them. We have caused irrevocable harm in the decimation of your faithful people. May we turn toward rooting out the hate and degradation that is seeded into our faith. May we turn toward repentance for the history of harm, and the present harm continually perpetuated against the Jewish people. May we stand in community with all your holy children, lifting them up, and use our privileges toward their flourishing.

Capitalism

It is utterly ridiculous
That a system touted as fair and just
Does so much damage to our world—
And so often under the guise of
    Your Holy Name.

God—how can such system continue to prosper
And hurt so many, lifting up so few
And the most marginalized continue to suffer
While the rich get richer?
How long, O Lord? Will we build false altars to
    wealth?
Where is the plague to wipe out this injustice,
And free us from its bonds?

Homelessness

Almighty Spirit,

Make us uncomfortable

When we pass by suffering.

Make us notice

Those we've labeled invisible.

Make us aware

Of the places we avoid.

Call us into the discomfort and dissonance

Of those who go without the most basic

Dignity of shelter and safety.

May we see the fullness of humanity of those
  without housing,

And recognize not their failings but our own.

Force us to see our complicity in their suffering,

And make their faces reflect our own.

Call us in—draw us close.

Turn our indignation toward the greed and
selfishness,

The structures of our society that allow so many
to suffer,

And start to build up their wholeness.

Patriarchy

Mother God

In our imposed silence

we burn

With the unspoken truths

Carried from generations to generation.

Fuel our voices

With an unquenchable thirst

For our voices to flow out

In every corner

In every industry

In every nation
May we reject our silencing,
Reclaim our power,
And hear Her holy voice
Urging us forward.

Violence against Women

For our bodies broken
So that others may feel power and pleasure,
We weep and we mourn.

For our souls violated
So that others may feel satisfied,
We weep and we mourn.

For our peace stolen
So that others may feel powerful,
We weep and we mourn.

For our justice denied
So that others may stay comfortable,
We rage.

For our integrity questioned
So that others may be unexamined.
We rage.

For their innocence assumed
So that they may be protected,
We rage.

For every violation endured that will never know
    justice
For every person who survives, for every person
    who does not,
We pray to you, Holy One. Hear our prayer.

Hunger

Despite the excess and abundance of the world,
So many go without, so many hunger and yearn
For the basic dignity of food.
For the disparities that sweep our world
Where children of God starve
While other children of God waste in excess,
We repent.
For greed, for our lack of humanity,
For every time we look away,
We repent.
For bellies that hunger,
We pray.

For caregivers desperate to provide,
We pray.

May we make no peace with a world that
hungers,
God forgive us.

Reproductive Rights

For the rights of our bodies, our families, and
    our destinies,
We pray.

For our foremothers whose bodies were not their
    own.
For our sisters who still fight for their choices,
We pray.

We pray and we demand—
With the voice of Mary's own consent
As the backbone of the Divine intention for
Us to have and to hold the rights over our own
    selves.

May our hope for the world root out
The corrosive control over bodies,
Another step toward justice
For those marginalized by the powerful.

May our autonomy be blessed,
May our autonomy be strengthened,
May our autonomy empower us
In our divine bodies to never
Relinquish that which is ours.

Ableism

Almighty God—

We've fallen short, in our ordering of the world,
　　to truly proclaim the diversity of your
　　creation—too often reducing one another
　　to our abilities to what can be capitalized
　　and given back into our human-made
　　machine of society.

May we tear down the structures that turn us
　　into commodities.
May we celebrate the fullness of human in every
　　body, every shape, every ability.
May we reject the sin of ableism, and root it out
　　from our way of being.

Help us root out our prejudice, our preconceived notions, and open our minds.

For those who break the mold, we pray.

For those who defy all expectations, we pray.

For the fullness of humanity, found in the presence of all bodies and abilities, we rejoice.

Indigenous People

Holy One—
We bear witness to the living peoples
Who first walked these lands, who cared for this
    Earth,
Who have known You and the sacredness of our
    existence from the beginning.

We bear witness to the violence,
The language, the land, the knowledge,
To all that has been stolen and slaughtered.

We do not turn away from the histories we share.
We do not recoil from our shared responsibility,
The harm, ancient and modern,
The children whose lives were stolen,

The missing and murdered indigenous women,
The land we continue to poison.

We bear the monumental weight of what cannot
    be undone or reclaimed
And we root ourselves toward a hope,
That in speaking truth and in bearing witness,
We may not repeat the sins of our ancestors,
And may take our steps toward repentance and
    repair.

Mental Healthcare

Into the cosmos I fling my lament against this
    thing that taunts and evades,
Wearing down my resolve and my soul,
And I weep for the mind that turns against itself
And our utter failure to truly heal those wounds.

For the extraordinary effort to hold tight to our
    love and commitment
In the face of ever mounting odds, we pray.

Whenever institution, safeguard, and potential
    hope falls short—
To where do I turn my laments? Where should I
    cast my pleas?

We have failed. And those of us left to pick up
    the pieces are too weary,
Our plates too full, our minds too stretched, to
    make it any better.
We bear witness to the failings around us,
And we cry out for ourselves, for those we love,
    for those we do not know.
We cry, we grieve, and we hold an unrelenting
    hope in something different.

Black Lives Matter

Holy One—

For the lives of all cannot matter
When the lives of some are slaughtered,
For holy Black lives, for holy Brown lives,
We pray.

For the lives stolen and the lives enslaved,
We repent—for Black lives are holy.

For the histories erased,
We remember—for Black lives are sacred.

May we stand against violence and vitriol,
May we clean our own house,
May we risk it all in the name of God's holy
children.

Healthcare Industry

For the commodification of compassion we weep,
For avoidable loss,
Unnecessary suffering,
For red tape and insurance forms, we lament
That our structure of care comes from a place of
    such scarcity.
When money is more valuable than life,
We grieve.

May we remember that we belong to one another
And that our mutual flourishing is priceless
And our compassion and care abundant and
    excessive.

LGBTQ+

Author of the universe—
Your creation has always existed within a
    complex beauty,
Reflecting the multifaceted nature of your very
    being,
Manifested so beautifully within humanity.

May our knowledge of you demand we
Know and see the reflection of your divinity
In all expressions of love, in all expressions of
    identity.

Unburden us from artificial restraints and
    definitions
That have only ever served to limit us.
Invite us into the full knowing of your holy
    creation
In all genders, in all expressions,
In all bonds of love, in all ways of being.

Renew our commitment to transforming the
    world,
Keep fast our hope in a future more loving and
    more diverse than we know,
Strengthen us that we may never compromise on
    the dignity and divinity
Of any of Your beloved and holy children.

Transgender

Despite the multitude of salutations we use
    for you,
Somehow we diminish one another to the
    simplicity of being
Something singularly defined and unchangeable

That we forget—
To be multifaceted is to be divine.

All too often it is the holiest parts of us
That we keep burning at the stake.

Petty
Rage

I f you want to learn how to pray—how to really pray with no inhibitions, ask children for their prayer requests. They will pray for anything and everything under the sun. In preschool chapel, children prayed for their toys, costumes, holiday presents, siblings, pets, and even once a giant squid.

Our faith doesn't have to be so serious, and our rage doesn't have to always be fully justified or valid. There are inane, ordinary, necessary, and daily occurrences that can invoke our internal fury like nothing else. While there may be a more enlightened way of living where these things don't hit a nerve, this is not that practice.

Repressing our feelings that we perceive as being "negative" does little to help our faith. In fact, we open ourselves to resentment and bitterness. We train ourselves to ignore and numb our feelings and thoughts. With the smallest of things, we shape our relationship and our authenticity with God. We influence how we perceive God to view us, and how we view ourselves. So instead of ignoring it, we acknowledge and move through even our pettiest rage. Nobody can rise above all the time. Sometimes we need to let it fall apart; sometimes we have nothing left to give. Sometimes we need to be selfish.

This is not permission for us to be judgmental or mean. This is not permission for us to disregard the feelings of others, or to just bypass accountability. But it's a place to briefly blow off some steam at the little things, so we can get back to what is really important.

We are allowed to rage about the little things. We are allowed to bring the small and the big to God. Compartmentalizing the little things, deeming them too ordinary or profane for our spiritual lives, reinforces the idea that only certain ways of being are allowed before God. The internalized shame we carry by thinking we should do better or be better just drives us further from the Divine.

This may be the place to begin our healing. If we stop asking ourselves if we are allowed to pray for something, if we stop forcing our conversation with God to look a certain way, if we stop needing a specific version of ourselves to show up, then we might discover something new. We might find our way to a new relationship with ourselves, and with the Divine we pray to. Let us rage.

Reply All

God—

When my email is full of unnecessary messages
I can understand why you sent the floods.

Might I suggest reply all—
As the next plague?

A constant loop of unnecessary information
Consuming our time?

Car Alarms

How long, O Lord?
Must we listen?

How long, O Lord?
Must we continue installing these?

How long, O Lord?
How long?

Traffic

Almighty God,

Does nobody else know how to use a turn signal?

Surely there cannot be this many idiotic people
   on the road.

—I JUST NEED TO GET WHERE I AM
   GOING.

Start the rapture, or whatever else will end this.

Daylight Savings

Divine Creator and Architect of the Universe,

In our awe of the wonders of your creation,

We reveal our arrogance,

Micromanaging even

Our perception

Of the turning of the earth

And squandering our collective energy

On antiquated efforts—

The epitome of the way we've always done it—

Forgive us for our failure to trust in you.

Late Fees

Holy One our Great Confessor,

Where is the grace that you teach us about?

Where is the compassion?

Fill the hearts of those who punish us—

With forgiving hearts

That we might be free from the consequences of
    our own actions.

May their spirits be moved to make me whole.

Auto-Renewals

God of All Things, it's as though these places
Don't truly care for me, and only care for money
They betray me, and turn against me
Chasing the false idol of ease, led into
    temptation,
Free me from the bondage of eternal
    subscriptions
That I may know a taste of the promised land.

Stuff

And more and more and more

The stuff that never ends

That seems to grow and multiply

Without purpose, but someone might use

Until it consumes both my space and my mind

And somehow I cannot be without

And more and more and more.

Holiness, from where does it all come?

The boxes and things and knick-knacks

And the stuff we hold dear and the things we

    don't remember

And every material good that we hope might be
A source of joy or happiness
Until it consumes me with rage because it is
Stuff and stuff and more stuff.

Holiness, free me from this stuff—
Expect a few things I might need,
Just in case.

Taxes

I cannot tell if I am more annoyed
By giving away my hard-earned money
On what I make and what I buy and what I sell
At every. Single. Turn.
Or by how difficult it is to even know the correct
    amount to give away
Or by how little the wealthiest contribute
And then I remember all the terrible things my
    money funds

And I am exhausted by how absolutely ridiculous
    this system is
And I am too tired and too busy to fix this
    system on top of everything else.
God, strike down the empire,
Preferably before April 15th.
Amen.

Spilled Milk

Why yes, I do want to cry over spilled milk,
To be angry and frustrated at yet another
    mess—
The things that fall apart and are left for me to
    clean up
When I do not have the time or energy or
    bandwidth,
The messes that are disgusting, and noticeable,
if they are cleaned wrong.
But what truly makes me seethe
Are these little jabs and sayings that have
Less to do with making our lives better
And more to do with controlling and contorting
Our feelings, just to make others feel better.
Fuck that.

Conclusion

Making It Your Own

It is daunting to step into the unknown and the unfamiliar. We have been trained to look for instructions so we know the right and wrong way to do things. Our faith is no different. Organized religions have often promoted a right way and a wrong way to practice faith. In fact, it's not only how religions and denominations have historically distinguished themselves, but also how identity and meaning have been formed for communities and cultures. Religion can be used as instrument of control, to further marginalize those who challenge establishment. It can become a barrier between people and God.

At their best, structure, form, and ritual can all have deeply meaningful and powerful places in our spiritual lives. Together, they become vehicles to connect our experiences to the Divine and to one another. Rage prayers can be a part of that formality, or they can lead you down new and unexplored paths. They are malleable and adaptive, a starting point and not the destination.

Rather than seeing these rage prayers as a prescriptive formula, let them be a springboard for your own expression to God. Let them inspire us to be vulnerable with God. Perhaps it will release a cathartic anger. Perhaps it will fill you with joy. It is not about bringing only the negative or the playful, but about bringing the authentic and unfiltered. They allow a certain curiosity and exploration of how we do things, and why. Let rage prayers help you explore a way of praying that is maybe different than what you've known before.

I recognize that my particular rage prayers found here will not speak to everyone. They are heavily influenced by my own specific experiences as a white Christian woman. I know my own context has given me privilege and bias that will not represent everyone. The language I use speaks to my own life and may not speak to everyone. We have seen time and again the failures of trying to make one voice speak for a group of people. Rather than find the universality, we can celebrate our particularities. Maybe that will mean the names for God are changed out for you. Maybe some prayers will not speak to your experience as they repent of sins that you do not identify with—or lament burdens you do not carry. So we take the parts that feel familiar, that speak to us and spark within us a desire to create something for ourselves or a different way of leaning into our spirituality. And it's ok to leave behind what does not serve our souls.

We are also compelled in this work to move through and beyond our thoughts and prayers, even when they are as authentic and meaningful as rage prayers. We do not wallow and stew forever in anger. Rage prayers are not permission to be stuck. Rage prayers are meant to help us move through our experiences and be in active, honest conversation with God. They are fuel to consume that which needs to be consumed, to push us forward to our next step. "Thoughts and prayers" are the starting place. They are what change us. What comes after is what changes the world.

With radical and ridiculous hope, I believe that shaking up our conversation with the Divine will give way to something beautiful and true. That our anger can have a sacred burn, and that more than anything God yearns for us to bring our whole, messy, authentic selves to our holy prayers.

Acknowledgments

I am deeply grateful to the people who made this book possible. To my editor and champion, Phil Marino, thank you for finding me, seeing something in *Rage Prayers*, and helping it become what it is today. Thank you to you and Laurie Harting for guiding me through this process with so much support and enthusiasm.

To my sister, Jenny, for your fierce loyalty, love, and support, I am eternally grateful. You have done more for me than I have words for, and I would not be the person I am today without you. To both you and Alan, thank you for loving me, supporting me, keeping me on my feet, and helping me step into this work. To my mom, Kay, and my stepdad, Dan, you are pillars of support that I am rarely deserving of, and nothing I have achieved would be possible without your love and presence. To my dad, Peter, may your memory be a blessing. I wish more than anything that you could read this.

To my friends who have cheered me along and helped make this book a reality: I owe deep gratitude and thanks to Chase for your love and for believing in me. Thank you to Angie for being there for me, for the cabin, and for always being a listening ear for my rage. To Audrey, your friendship and love is unmatched. The support from you, Taline, and Jaimie keeps me going. You three are badass, extraordinary women, and I am in awe of all of you. To Callie, my coach and dear friend, for our wisdom and steadiness, thank you.

To the people who saw me at fifteen and encouraged me to pursue my calling I give my deep gratitude and love. For the community of St. Mary's Episcopal Church in Anchorage and the Diocese of Alaska, Rev. Micheal Burke, Rev. Katherine Hunt, Maggie Wilkinson, Sarah Stanley, Rev. Hunter Silides, Tricia Grenier, and the blessed memories of Charles Jackson and the Rev. Connie Jones.

I would not have this opportunity without the community of creators and followers on TikTok. To all of you who have shown up there—to my fellow creators of #progressiveclergy—and everyone who has engaged with that work, thank you.

Finally, to my children, thank you. Eleanor, Amelia, and Peter, you are my greatest inspiration and my deepest joy. Knowing and loving you has brought me into a deeper understanding of God than I could have ever imagined. I love you three so much, and I hope and pray you each find your voice and your unique connection to the Divine.